EYEWITNESS PROJECT BOOKS
DINOSAURS
by Claire Watts

LONDON, NEW YORK,
MELBOURNE, MUNICH, AND DELHI

Educational Consultants Linda B. Gambrell
and Geraldine Taylor

Senior Editor Susan Reuben
Assistant Editor Lisa Stock
Art Editor Peter Laws
Managing Art Editor Owen Peyton Jones
Managing Editor Camilla Hallinan
Art Director Martin Wilson
Publishing Manager Sunita Gahir
Category Publisher Andrea Pinnington
DK Picture Library Claire Bowers, Lucy Claxton,
Rose Horridge, Myriam Megharbi, Romaine Werblow
Production Editor Hitesh Patel
Senior Production Controller Man Fai Lau
Jacket Designer Andy Smith

DK Delhi
Art Director Shefali Upadhyay
Designer Govind Mittal
DTP Designers Harish Aggarwal, Dheeraj Arora

First published in Great Britain in 2008 by
Dorling Kindersley Limited,
80 Strand, London WC2R 0RL

Copyright © 2008 Dorling Kindersley Limited
A Penguin Company

2 4 6 8 10 9 7 5 3 1
ED687 – 04/08

A CIP catalogue record for this book
is available from the British Library.

ISBN: 978-1-40533-130-2

Colour reproduction by Colourscan, Singapore
Printed and bound by L.Rex Printing Co. Ltd

**Discover more at
www.dk.com**

Contents

4   How this book can help your child

Fast facts

6   What is a dinosaur?

7   Dinosaur world

8   Carnivores

9   Herbivores

10   Dinosaur defence

11   Dinosaur families

12   Discovering dinosaurs

13   End of the dinosaurs

Activities

14 The birth of the dinosaurs
15 Classifying dinosaurs
16 The age of the dinosaurs
18 Herbivores and carnivores
19 Dinosaur bodies
20 Hands and feet
22 Defence and adornment
24 Land of the dinosaurs
26 Hunting and scavenging
27 Grazing dinosaurs
28 Birth and growth
30 Other prehistoric creatures
32 Dinosaur discoveries
33 Fossils
34 How to rebuild a dinosaur
36 From dinosaur to bird
37 End of the dinosaur age

Quick quiz

38 Dinosaur bodies
39 Mesozoic world
40 Attack and defence
41 Dinosaur lives
42 Fossil finding
43 Dinosaur destruction

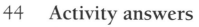

44 **Activity answers**
46 **Quick quiz answers**
47 **Progress chart**
48 **Certificate**

Back-cover chart
    Dinosaur facts
    Dinosaur discoveries

How this book can help your child

Eyewitness Project Books offer a fun and colourful range of stimulating titles in the subjects of history, science, and geography. Specially designed to appeal to children of 8 years and up, each project book aims to:

- develop a child's knowledge of a popular topic
- provide practice of key skills and reinforce classroom learning
- nurture a child's special interest in a subject.

The series is devised and written with the expert advice of educational and reading consultants, and supports the school curriculum.

About this book

Eyewitness Project Book Dinosaurs is an activity-packed exploration of dinosaurs and their prehistoric world. Inside you will find:

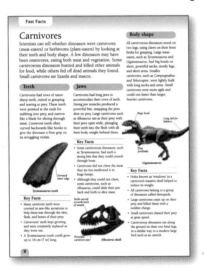

Fast facts

This section presents key information as concise facts, which are easy to digest, learn, and remember. Encourage your child to start by reading through the valuable information in the Fast facts section and studying the statistics chart inside the flap at the back of the book before trying out the activities.

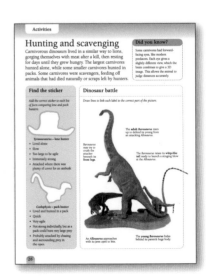

The enjoyable, fill-in activities are designed to develop information recall and help your child practise cross-referencing skills. Each activity can be completed using information provided on the page, in the Fast facts section, or on the back-cover chart. Your child should work systematically through the book and tackle just one or two activity topics in a session. Encourage your child by checking answers together and offering extra guidance when necessary.

Quick quiz

There are six pages of multiple-choice questions to test your child's new-found knowledge of the subject. Children should only try answering the quiz questions once all of the activity section has been completed. As your child finishes each page of themed questions, check the answers together.

Answers and Progress chart

All the answers are supplied in full at the back of the book, so no prior knowledge of the subject is required.

Use the Progress chart to motivate your child and be positive about his or her achievements. On the completion of each activity or quiz topic, reward good work with a gold star.

Certificate

There is a Certificate of excellence at the back of the book for your child to fill in, remove, and display on the wall.

Lift the flap

The chart inside the back cover is a fun learning tool, packed with fascinating facts and figures about dinosaurs. Happy learning!

Important information

Please ensure that your child wears gloves and goggles when handling the Epsom salts in the fossil activity on page 33. All other activities in this book can be carried out without adult supervision.

What is a dinosaur?

For more than 150 million years, hundreds of species of dinosaur roamed Earth, spreading over every habitat that existed on the land. Today, there are no living dinosaurs, but we know about them because their bones and other remains have been preserved in rock as fossils.

Shape and size

Solid, column-like legs

Model of *Barosaurus*

Dinosaur definition

A dinosaur is a member of a group of reptiles which once lived on the land but which are now all extinct (no longer living). Like other reptiles, such as snakes and lizards, dinosaurs were animals with backbones and they laid eggs, rather than giving birth to live young.

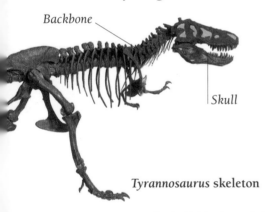

Backbone

Skull

***Tyrannosaurus* skeleton**

Key Facts

- All dinosaurs were land animals; flying and swimming reptiles that existed at the same time were not dinosaurs.
- Modern reptiles are cold-blooded, but scientists cannot agree whether dinosaurs were cold- or warm-blooded.
- Most dinosaurs had dry, scaly or armoured skin, but some had feathers.

Dinosaur legs

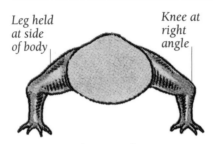

Leg held at side of body

Knee at right angle

Sprawling reptile stance

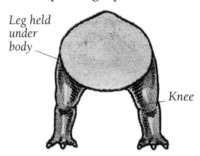

Leg held under body

Knee

Erect stance of dinosaur

All dinosaurs had straight legs tucked under their bodies, like modern mammals, rather than sprawling legs at the sides like other reptiles. This more upright stance meant that dinosaurs could move more efficiently than other reptiles and so they developed more active lifestyles.

Key Facts

- A dinosaur's weight was supported on top of its legs, like pillars supporting a building.
- Other reptiles use muscle power to suspend their body weight as they move.

Smaller forelimbs

Muscular back legs

Model of *Hysilophodon*

The smallest dinosaurs were bird-like creatures about the size of a chicken, while the biggest weighed up to 50 tonnes, as much as ten African elephants. Some dinosaurs moved on four legs, while other dinosaurs moved on two muscular back legs, using their front legs to grasp vegetation or prey.

Key Facts

- The largest dinosaurs were all herbivores (plant-eaters).
- About 700 species of dinosaur have been named, but half are based on incomplete skeletons, so may not be separate species.
- Some scientists believe there may be another 800 dinosaur genera (closely related species) yet to be discovered.
- Dinosaurs had much longer legs in comparison to their body size than other reptiles.
- Dinosaurs walked on their toes, as birds do.

Dinosaur world

During the time that dinosaurs existed, the world around them changed. The climate varied, different plants and animals evolved (gradually developed), the landscape was changed by geological forces such as volcanic activity and erosion, and even the continents shifted their positions. Different species of dinosaur evolved to live in different environments.

When

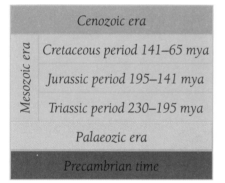

Cenozoic era	
	Cretaceous period 141–65 mya
Mesozoic era	Jurassic period 195–141 mya
	Triassic period 230–195 mya
Palaeozic era	
Precambrian time	

Scientists divide Earth's past into sections called eras. The Mesozoic era, from between 230 mya (million years ago) and 65 mya, is sometimes known as the age of the dinosaurs, because dinosaurs were the dominant animals during this period. The Mesozoic is divided into three smaller sections, called periods: the Triassic, the Jurassic, and the Cretaceous.

Key Facts

- During the Triassic, the first dinosaurs evolved.
- During the Jurassic, huge herbivorous dinosaurs dominated life on land.
- During the Cretaceous, dinosaurs on different continents evolved separately, leading to many different species.

Plant life

During the Triassic, the landscape was dominated by evergreen shrubs and trees. During the Jurassic, huge areas of tropical forest containing conifers and cycads grew, with ferns covering the ground. In the Cretaceous, the first flowering plants appeared. At first these were tiny low-growing plants, but gradually they evolved into large forests.

Key Facts

- During the Triassic, conditions on Earth were warm and dry.
- During the Jurassic, temperatures fell and there was more rainfall.
- During the Cretaceous, the climate developed seasonal changes and world climates varied more.

Cycad

Continental drift

At the beginning of the Mesozoic, all the continents on Earth were joined in one great landmass. Over the next 150 million years, the continents gradually drifted apart. As the continents moved, Earth's climate changed and sea levels rose and fell. New forms of animals and plants evolved which were adapted to the new conditions.

TRIASSIC

JURASSIC

CRETACEOUS

Position of landmasses during the Mesozoic

Key Facts

- During the Triassic, all land on Earth was joined in a supercontinent called Pangea.
- During the Jurassic, Pangea split into several continents.
- During the Cretaceous, the continents split further, drifting to their present-day positions.

Carnivores

Scientists can tell whether dinosaurs were carnivores (meat-eaters) or herbivores (plant-eaters) by looking at their teeth and body shape. A few dinosaurs may have been omnivores, eating both meat and vegetation. Some carnivorous dinosaurs hunted and killed other animals for food, while others fed off dead animals they found. Small carnivores ate lizards and insects.

Teeth

Carnivores had rows of razor-sharp teeth, suited to grasping and tearing at prey. These teeth were pointed at the ends for stabbing into prey, and narrow like a blade for slicing through meat. Carnivore teeth often curved backwards like hooks to give the dinosaur a firm grip on its struggling victim.

Serrated inner edge

Tyrannosaurus tooth

Key Facts

- Many carnivore teeth were covered in saw-like serrations to help them tear through the skin, flesh, and bones of their prey.
- Carnivores' teeth kept growing and were constantly replaced as they wore out.
- A *Tyrannosaurus* tooth could grow up to 18 cm (7 in) long.

Jaws

Carnivores had long jaws to accommodate their rows of teeth. Strong jaw muscles produced a powerful bite, snapping the jaws shut on prey. Large carnivores such as *Allosaurus* ran at their prey with their jaws open wide, plunging their teeth into the flesh with all their body weight behind them.

Key Facts

- Some carnivorous dinosaurs, such as *Tyrannosaurus*, had such a strong bite that they could crunch through bone.
- Carnivores did not chew the meat they ate but swallowed it in huge lumps.
- Although they could not chew, some carnivores, such as *Allosaurus*, could slide their jaw back and forth to slice meat.

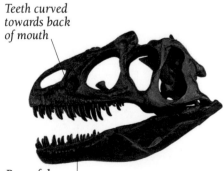

Teeth curved towards back of mouth

Powerful carnivore jaw

Allosaurus skull

Body shape

All carnivorous dinosaurs stood on two legs, using claws on their front limbs for grasping. Large meat-eaters, such as *Tyrannosaurus* and *Giganotosaurus*, had big heads on short, powerful necks, sturdy legs, and short arms. Smaller carnivores, such as *Compsognathus* and *Velociraptor*, were lightly built with long necks and arms. Small carnivores were more agile and could run faster than larger, heavier carnivores.

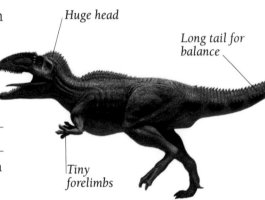

Huge head

Long tail for balance

Tiny forelimbs

Giganotosaurus

Key Facts

- Holes known as 'windows' in a carnivore's massive skull helped to reduce its weight.
- All carnivores belong to a group of dinosaurs called theropods.
- Large carnivores crept up on their prey and killed them with a sudden charge.
- Small carnivores chased their prey at great speed.
- Carnivorous dinosaurs ran along the ground on their two hind legs, in a similar way to a modern large bird such as an ostrich.

Herbivores

There were far more herbivores than carnivores in the dinosaur world. Giant herbivores fed off the highest treetops, while smaller herbivores grazed on shrubs and ground-dwelling plants. The biggest herbivores, such as *Brachiosaurus* and *Diplodocus*, had to eat almost all the time to get enough food to fuel their giant bodies.

Teeth

Herbivore teeth came in different shapes depending on the dinosaur's way of eating. Thin, peg-like teeth were used to rake in vegetation. Sharp, spoon-shaped teeth were used for nipping off plants. Some dinosaurs had rows of sharp flat teeth which ground and chopped material before it was swallowed, while others swallowed without chewing.

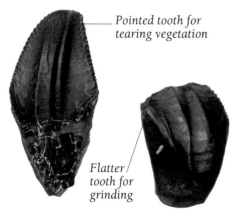

Pointed tooth for tearing vegetation

Flatter tooth for grinding

Iguanodon teeth

Key Facts

- Some herbivores had up to 960 tightly-packed teeth.
- Dinosaurs that did not chew their food had no teeth at the back of their mouths.
- No dinosaur had flat teeth like human molars which we use to grind and crush food.

Jaws

Most herbivores had lighter jaws with weaker muscles than the big carnivores. Raking in or nipping off vegetation requires much less strength than having to hold onto struggling prey. Most reptiles have no cheeks. Their mouth opening extends right to their jaws. However almost all herbivorous dinosaurs had cheeks which helped them hold food in their mouths while they chewed it.

Key Facts

- Some herbivores, such as *Iguanodon*, had no front teeth. Instead, they had a beak which they used to scoop up vegetation.
- The beaks of hadrosaurs, or duck-billed dinosaurs, were wide and flat like a duck's beak.
- Some dinosaurs, such as *Edmontosaurus*, had a hinged upper jaw which moved outwards as it closed, grinding the back teeth over one another.

Wide and flat beak

Long, flat jaw

Iguanodon skull

Body shape

Herbivores had different body shapes to suit their differing diets. Massive herbivores, such as *Barosaurus*, had long, flexible necks and small light heads so they could reach up to the treetops. Stocky herbivores, such as *Triceratops*, had strong, thick necks for wrenching at tough vegetation.

Long neck to reach highest tree branches

Barosaurus

Key Facts

- Most herbivores moved on four legs, but some may have been able to rear up on their hind legs.
- Long-necked herbivores, such as *Barosaurus*, walked with their tails raised, counterbalancing the weight of their necks.
- Some herbivores, such as *Iguanodon*, grazed on four legs but ran on two back legs.

Dinosaur defence

Herbivorous dinosaurs were always at risk from attack by carnivores and needed to protect themselves. For the largest herbivores, their sheer size made them difficult for most carnivores to attack. Smaller, lighter dinosaurs could run away at great speed. Many herbivores evolved amazing defensive body parts, such as armour, horns, or spiked or whip-like tails.

Horns

Bony frill *Three horns*

Triceratops

Some dinosaurs had horns on their noses or over their eyes. These dinosaurs used their horns both to defend themselves against attackers, and to fight members of their own species for rights to territory or mates, as horned animals do today. They fought by charging with their heads lowered and horns pointing forwards.

Key Facts

• Horned dinosaurs belong to a group called ceratopsians.
• Ceratopsians had large bony frills pointing backwards from their skulls to mask their necks.
• Ceratopsians did not have armour on their bodies.

Plates

Some dinosaurs, such as *Euoplocephalus*, had flat, bony plates embedded in their skin and covered in horn. These plates, called scutes, protected them from the sharp teeth and claws of predators. When they were attacked, armoured dinosaurs probably crouched on the ground to protect their soft underparts.

Key Facts

• Armoured dinosaurs belong to a group called anklyosaurs.
• Big anklyosaurs even had armoured eyelids.
• All armoured or horned dinosaurs were heavy and walked on four legs, as a rhinoceros does.

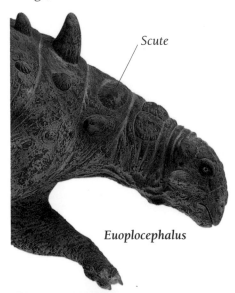

Scute

Euoplocephalus

Spikes

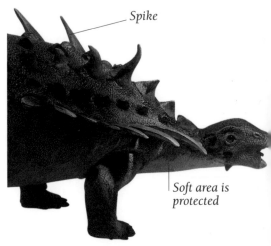

Spike

Soft area is protected

Gastonia

Some dinosaurs had spikes around their necks or flanks or all over their bodies except their bellies. These formed formidable weapons in a fight, when they could be driven into the skin of an attacker. Some dinosaurs, such as *Stegosaurus*, had spikes at the end of their tails which they could lash about to fight back against a predator.

Key Facts

• The spikes were made of bone and covered with smooth horn.
• The bone core of the spike was attached to the dinosaur's skin, not to its skeleton.
• Spikes on a dinosaur's neck or flank protected the softest parts of its body from attackers.
• These spikes made it hard for a predator to bite the dinosaur without injuring its own mouth.
• *Gastonia* had spikes all over its body and tail, like a walking thorn bush.
• *Edmontonia* had long bony spikes projecting from its shoulders which it could thrust into the leg of an attacking carnivore, giving it a severe wound.

Dinosaur families

Some dinosaurs lived together in family groups, while others, such as large carnivores like *Tyrannosaurus*, lived alone. But even *Tyrannosaurus* must have come together with members of its own species to mate. Some dinosaurs, such as *Troodon* and *Maiasaura*, gathered in colonies at breeding times, to nest and raise their young.

Living together

Some herbivores, such as *Maiasaura* and *Triceratops*, lived in herds. Being in a herd provides protection for each individual, as it is difficult for a predator to pick off one animal from the herd to kill. Many carnivores, such as *Allosaurus* or *Deinonychus*, may have lived and hunted in packs.

Eggs

Dinosaur eggs were hard and brittle like birds' eggs rather than soft and leathery like the eggs of other reptiles. Massive dinosaurs did not lay huge eggs in proportion to their size. The shell of such large eggs would have been too thick for oxygen to pass through and the baby would have been unable to break the shell easily to hatch out.

Shell cracked during fossilization

Oviraptor egg

Key Facts

- More than 200 dinosaur egg sites have been found.
- Dinosaur eggs come in different shapes: spherical, elongated, or shaped like a bird's egg.
- The largest dinosaur eggs that have been found are 60 cm (2 ft) long.

Caring for young

Young dinosaurs emerging from eggs

Protoceratops

Dinosaurs laid their eggs in nests scraped in the earth. Some dinosaurs sat on their nests to incubate their eggs. After the eggs hatched, some adults cared for the hatchlings, bringing food to them in the nest, until they were able to fend for themselves.

Key Facts

- Crushed eggshell in a dinosaur nest shows that the hatchlings stayed in the nest for some time after hatching, breaking the shell underfoot.
- Eggs that are broken only at the top where the young emerged show that the hatchlings left the nest soon after hatching.
- Some carnivorous dinosaurs ate the young of their own species.

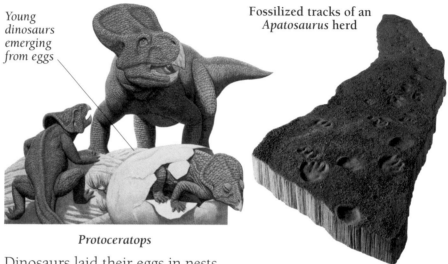

Fossilized tracks of an Apatosaurus herd

Key Facts

- We know that some dinosaurs travelled in groups because large clusters of fossil bones and footprints have been found together.
- Herbivores may have made seasonal migrations across vast distances in search of grazing land and breeding sites.
- Young dinosaurs would have walked in the centre of the herd, protected by the adults around them.
- Carnivores that worked together as a pack were the most intelligent of the dinosaurs.
- Pack hunters would have shared the kill, as lions do.

Discovering dinosaurs

When a dinosaur died, if its body was immediately buried in the right conditions, it might turn into a fossil. However, very few prehistoric animals became fossilized, and only a tiny fraction of those fossils has been found. Scientists investigate fossil finds to build up a picture of the age of the dinosaurs.

Fossils

Fossils are the remains or traces of plants and animals that were once living which have been preserved as rock. A fossil may be a cast, where the rock has formed an exact replica of an object such as a bone, or an impression, such as a footprint or a leaf print.

Key Facts

- Body fossils are remains of plants and animals.
- Trace fossils are traces left behind, such as footprints, nests, and droppings.
- Fossils are harder and heavier than the original materials.
- Pressure within the rocks may alter the position and shape of fossils, making it difficult for experts to work out what shape they were originally.

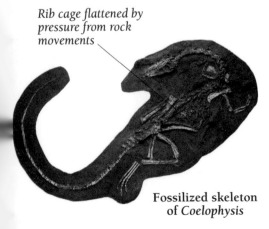

Rib cage flattened by pressure from rock movements

Fossilized skeleton of *Coelophysis*

Palaeontology

Dental drill

Fossils are freed from rock with fine tools

The study of fossils is called palaeontology. Palaeontologists excavate fossils, then compare them to other fossils and to modern plants and animals. This helps them work out the former appearance and lifestyle of extinct plants and animals.

Key Facts

- Most fossils are found when the rock around them is eroded and they come to the surface naturally. So coastlines and deserts, where there is continual erosion with wind and water, are good fossil-hunting sites.
- Palaeontologists study not just the fossils but the site where they are found for clues about the life of the animal or plant.

Fossilization

Struthiomimus lies dead on a river bank.

Struthiomimus is buried by mud and silt.

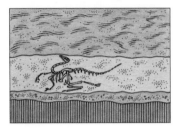

After millions of years, the fossilized skeleton of Struthiomimus is exposed by movements of the rocks.

The process of fossilization

If a dinosaur was buried in mud or sand after its death, the soft parts of its body rotted away. Over thousands of years, the mud or sand turned to rock. Water seeping through the skeleton destroyed the bones, replacing them with minerals and turning them into rock. These rocks retain the shape of the original bones and are called fossils.

Key Facts

- An entire dinosaur skeleton only survives as a fossil if it is buried immediately and not torn apart by scavengers.
- The most common fossils are teeth, as they are very hard.

End of the dinosaurs

All the dinosaurs died out by the end of the Cretaceous 65 million years ago. It is possible that the dinosaurs became extinct slowly as they were unable to adapt to changes in the environment. But most scientists believe that the end of the dinosaurs was much more sudden, brought about by a catastrophic event.

Mass extinction

A whole range of creatures died out at the same time, including all the pterosaurs (flying reptiles). Many ocean creatures became extinct, including all marine reptiles except turtles. Other land reptiles, such as crocodiles, survived, as did birds, amphibians, and mammals. Many plants also became extinct.

Key Facts

• Fossil records cannot tell us whether the extinction happened over weeks or hundreds of years.

• Dinosaurs appear to have been in decline around five million years before they became extinct.

Large crest on head

Corythosaurus, a late Cretaceous dinosaur

Meteorite impact

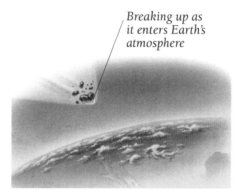

Breaking up as it enters Earth's atmosphere

Meteorite heading for Mexican coast

The most widely accepted theory is that a massive meteorite (rock from space) hit Earth, throwing a cloud of dust into the atmosphere which blocked out the Sun's light for years. Without sunlight, plants died; animals that fed on plants had no food and so they died; and carnivores had no prey so they died.

Key Facts

• In 1990, a huge meteorite crater 180 km (110 miles) across was discovered in the seabed off the coast of Yucatán, Mexico.

• The meteorite would have measured 10 km (6 miles) across.

• It struck Earth at a speed of 100,000 kph (62,000 mph).

• Scientists have dated this meteorite to about 65 million years ago.

Dinosaur descendants

Scientists believe that small meat-eating dinosaurs evolved into birds. Some of these dinosaurs developed feathers, possibly to help keep the dinosaurs warm. The earliest birds retained dinosaur features such as claws on the front of their wings, and teeth in their beaks. They probably climbed up trees with their claws and then fluttered down.

Claws on wings

Archaeopteryx

Key Facts

• The earliest true bird is *Archaeopteryx* which lived during the late Jurassic, at the same time as dinosaurs.

• All birds have a wishbone to keep their wing joint in place; some meat-eating dinosaurs also had this bone.

• Early birds had a long, bony tail like a dinosaur, rather than a short stump of bone like modern birds.

• Modern lizards are not descendants of dinosaurs. They evolved at the same time as dinosaurs, but did not die out at the end of the Cretaceous.

• Crocodiles are the nearest living reptile relatives of dinosaurs.

The birth of the dinosaurs

Dinosaurs belong to a group of animals called archosaurs, which means 'ruling reptiles'. This group includes crocodiles and pterosaurs (flying reptiles). Dinosaurs lived on Earth for 165 million years, with new species evolving as the world around them changed. We human beings have only existed for about 100,000 years.

Did you know?

More species of dinosaurs existed during the late Cretaceous period than in all of the rest of dinosaur history put together.

How dinosaurs evolved

Use the information below to number the pictures in the right order to show how dinosaurs evolved.

1. The earliest archosaurs were crocodile-like carnivorous reptiles called thecodontians. They spent most of their time in water but could also move on land.

2. During the Triassic, some tiny thecodontians grew more agile, with legs tucked under their bodies rather than sprawling legs. They left the water to live on land, but they still walked on all fours.

3. Some thecodontians began to walk on two legs on the land. They held their spines horizontally rather than upright like a two-legged dinosaur.

4. The earliest dinosaurs had a more upright gait, and so moved faster than the thecodontians, and could use their forelimbs for grasping.

a.

b.

Evolution of dinosaurs

c.

d.

Evolution clock

Follow the instructions below to represent Earth's history in the space of an hour, comparing the age of the dinosaurs with the age of human beings.
In this diagram, 1 hour = 4.6 billion years and 1 minute = 76.6 million years.

1 Draw a line from the clock's centre to the 12. Next to this, write "Earth formed 4.6 billion years ago".

2 Draw a line from the centre to the 20-minute point. Write next to this "Earliest life formed 3.8 billion years ago".

3 Draw lines from the centre to the 57- and 59-minute points. Label this section "Age of the dinosaurs, 228 mya to 65 mya".

4 Draw the thinnest line you can to the left of the line you drew in step 1, to represent just a few seconds. Write next to this "Humans evolved 2.2 mya".

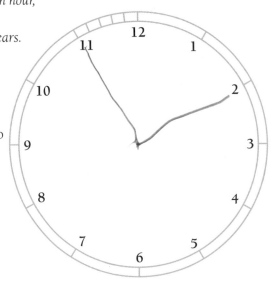

Classifying dinosaurs

Dinosaurs are classified into different groups according to common characteristics, such as similar appearance, way of moving, or lifestyle. When new species of dinosaur are discovered, scientists invent names for them made up of ancient Greek or Latin words. These names may describe a feature of their bodies, the place they were found, or a person involved in their discovery.

Classification facts

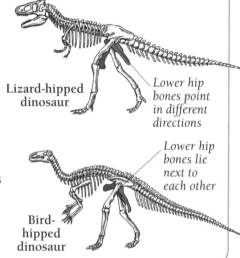

- The two main groups of dinosaurs are classified according to the structure of their hip bones.

- Saurischian or lizard-hipped dinosaurs had hips in which two lower bones pointed in opposite directions.

- Ornithischian or bird-hipped dinosaurs had two lower hip bones lying together behind the back leg.

- Ornithischians were all herbivores.

Lizard-hipped dinosaur — Lower hip bones point in different directions

Lower hip bones lie next to each other — **Bird-hipped dinosaur**

True or false?

Read the following statements about dinosaur groups and names. Use the information on this page to work out which statements are true and which are false and then tick the correct boxes.

	TRUE	FALSE
1. Scientists divide dinosaurs into two main groups, depending on the shape of their skulls.	☐	☐
2. Saurischian dinosaurs are also known as lizard-hipped dinosaurs.	☐	☐
3. All ornithischian dinosaurs ate birds.	☐	☐
4. Dinosaur names are made up of ancient Greek and Latin words.	☐	☐
5. Dinosaurs are sometimes named after the person who found them.	☐	☐
6. Ornithischian dinosaurs had hip bones which pointed in opposite directions.	☐	☐

Name the dinosaurs

Look at the dinosaur pictures, then number the table to match each dinosaur with the translation of its name.

Bony frill
Brow horns
Nose horn

1. *Triceratops*

Beak-like bone

Teeth at back of mouth

2. *Psittacosaurus*

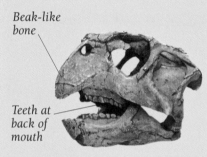

Blade-like carnivore teeth

Huge, curved claws

3. *Deinonychus*

No.	Translation
	"terrible claw"
	"parrot lizard"
	"three-horned face"

The age of the dinosaurs

As the environment changed during the Mesozoic era, new species of animals and plants evolved to survive in the different conditions, and some older species became extinct. During the Triassic, there were few different types of dinosaurs, but by the end of the Cretaceous an enormous variety of dinosaurs had evolved, each suited to its particular habitat or diet.

Dinosaur times

Use the information on page 7 to fill in the missing dates, and your back-cover chart to fill in the missing dinosaur names. Then find three landmass stickers and three dinosaur stickers to put in the correct picture spaces.

Triassic period

.... mya

All land was joined together as one great landmass, Pangea.

Similar types of dinosaurs lived throughout the whole of Pangea.

Jurassic period

.... mya

Pangea split apart.

Lush vegetation gave rise to giant herbivorous dinosaurs, including ...., the largest dinosaur that ever existed.

Cretaceous period .... mya

The continents split further apart, beginning the formation of the present-day continents.

During the Cretaceous, dinosaurs on different continents evolved separately, so dinosaurs in one part of the world were different from those elsewhere.

Cretaceous herbivores, such as *Corythosaurus*, could move on two legs or four.

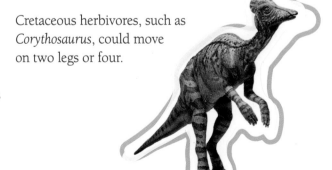

Did you know?

During the age of the dinosaurs, there were no other land-based creatures bigger than a domestic cat. The tiny mammals that existed were probably nocturnal, to keep out of the way of the voracious carnivorous dinosaurs.

The earliest known dinosaur was

....

Early herbivores such as *Plateosaurus* ate scrubby semi-desert plants.

In proportion to its overall size, *Stegosaurus* had the smallest brain of any dinosaur: about the size of a walnut.

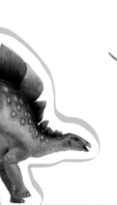

Chicken-sized carnivore *Compsognathus* ate tiny reptiles and insects.

The first flowering plants appeared during the Cretaceous.

....

is the biggest carnivore that has ever been discovered.

Cretaceous carnivore .... is the smallest dinosaur ever found at just 77 cm (30 in) long.

The age of the dinosaurs ended suddenly, possibly due to the impact of a massive meteorite.

Herbivores and carnivores

Different species of animals are linked in a food chain that connects predators (hunters) with their prey (the animals they eat). At the bottom of the dinosaur food chain are the herbivores which are the prey of carnivores. At the top, the large carnivorous dinosaurs have no predators but may be eaten by scavengers when they are dead.

Did you know?

Palaeontologists study coprolites (fossilized dung) to find out what the dinosaurs ate. They contain undigested food fragments such as bones, or plant remains.

Coprolite

Dinosaur differences

Use the information on pages 8 and 9 to help you decide which column is about carnivores and which is about herbivores and label them. Add two stickers in the picture spaces. Then use your back-cover chart to add some examples of herbivores and carnivores to the bottom of the table. Choose from:

Allosaurus   Brachiosaurus   Eoraptor   Iguanodon   Plateosaurus   Tyrannosaurus

Seismosaurus

Carnotaurus

Carnivore/ Herbivore		
Diet	meat	plants
Teeth	razor-sharp, often curved	peg-like, spoon-shaped, or flat
Jaws	long, with strong muscles	usually light with weaker muscles
Movement	walked or ran on two legs	some on two legs; others on four legs
Triassic example		
Jurassic example		
Cretaceous example		

Dinosaur bodies

Although dinosaur skin usually rots away with other soft parts before fossilization happens, palaeontologists have found a few examples which show the texture of the skin. However, it is impossible to tell what colour dinosaurs were because during fossilization, the skin is transformed into rock and loses its original colour.

Dinosaur skin

Number each caption to match the correct picture.

☐ Fossil evidence shows that some small predators, such as *Velociraptor*, had **feathers**.

☐ Dinosaur skin may have been **covered in patterns** to camouflage them against vegetation or other members of the herd.

☐ Most dinosaurs had skin covered in **pebbly scales** the size of peas.

☐ Some dinosaurs had rows of **flexible armoured plates** running along their bodies.

1.

2.

3.

4.

How big were dinosaurs?

These dinosaur silhouettes are shown next to a human figure to show you how big they were. Name the dinosaurs by comparing their sizes to the information on your back-cover chart. Choose from:

Brachiosaurus   Compsognathus   Tyrannosaurus

1.

2.

3.

Length: 1.4 m (4 ft 6 in)
Name: ....

Length: 12 m (39 ft)
Name: ....

Length: 25 m (82 ft)
Name: ....

Hands and feet

Some dinosaurs used all four limbs for walking on, some used their forelimbs as arms, while others could walk either on all fours or on two legs. Dinosaur claws were different shapes depending on their function. Carnivores had sharp, curved claws for killing prey. Herbivores usually had broader, flatter claws.

Did you know?

Tyrannosaurus had forelimbs no longer than an adult man's arms. It could not even reach its own mouth when feeding.

Walking and grasping

Look at the pictures and the labels carefully. Number each label to match the correct part of one of these pictures. Then tick a box under each picture to show if it is a hand or a foot. Remember that some dinosaurs used their hands for walking as well as grasping.

1 **Iguanodon**

Four powerful but inflexible toes to support heavy body as it walked.

Small first toe would not have reached the ground

Strong, broad foot suited to heavy plodding walk

Three forward pointing hoof-like toes for walking on

Solid, inflexible thumb spike for defence

Flexible, jointed fifth finger for grasping vegetation

3

2

Hand ☐

Foot ☐

5

4

6

Hand ☐

Foot ☐

Scelidosaurus

Dinosaur hands

Dinosaur hands were not as flexible as yours. Try this test to see what Iguanodon *could pick up with its hands. You need:*

• *bandage* • *safety pin* • *objects of different sizes and shapes, such as a stick, a ball, a marble, a sponge, a piece of cloth* • *helper*

1 To make your hand work like *Iguanodon*'s five-fingered hand, ask someone to bandage your three middle fingers together and bandage your thumb so that it sticks out from your hand and cannot bend.

2 Lay out the objects. Which objects can you pick up?

....
....
....
....
....
....

3 Which of your fingers can you use to grasp objects?

....

Claws

Add the correct words to complete the captions, using the pictures to help you. Choose from:

curved   knuckles   digging   slashing

1.

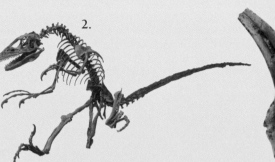
2.

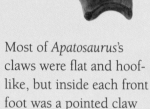
3.

4.

Therizinosaurus had such long claws that it probably had to walk on its ....

On its second toe, *Deinonychus* had a deadly claw that was twice as long as all its other claws, for .... at prey.

Most of *Apatosaurus*'s claws were flat and hoof-like, but inside each front foot was a pointed claw probably for ....

Baryonyx had huge, ... claws like hooks on its hands, which may have been used to catch fish.

Movement puzzle

Circle the correct word to complete each sentence about movement. Use the information on this page and on pages 8 and 9 to help you.

Hadrosaurus

Brachiosaurus

1. All **carnivores / herbivores** walked on two legs.
2. Large herbivores such as *Brachiosaurus* could rear up on their hind legs using their **necks / tails** for balance.
3. *Brachiosaurus / Tyrannosaurus / Gallimimus* could run at speeds of up to 80 kph (50 mph).
4. *Scelidosaurus / Hadrosaurus / Iguanodon* had a thumb spike.
5. Herbivores such as *Apatosaurus* may have used their sharpest claws for **cracking eggs / digging / killing prey**.

Movement facts

- The fastest dinosaurs, such as *Gallimimus*, could sprint at speeds of up to 80 kph (50 mph) – faster than a racehorse.

- Huge carnivores, such as *Tyrannosaurus*, may have been able to run a short distance at up to 36 kph (23 mph).

- Giant herbivores, such as *Brachiosaurus*, probably moved at about 6 kph (3.5 mph), about the same as human walking pace.

- When heavy herbivores such as *Barosaurus* reared up on their hind legs to feed on high branches, they leaned back on their massive, muscular tails for balance.

Defence and adornment

Some herbivores evolved specialized body parts, which could be used as weapons to defend themselves, or body armour to protect themselves from attackers. Other unusual body parts, such as bony bumps, spikes, and crests on the head, made individual dinosaurs stand out in the mating season, helping them attract a mate.

Did you know?

With its three horns and massive frill, *Triceratops'* head took up one third of its entire body length.

Triceratops

Tail weapons

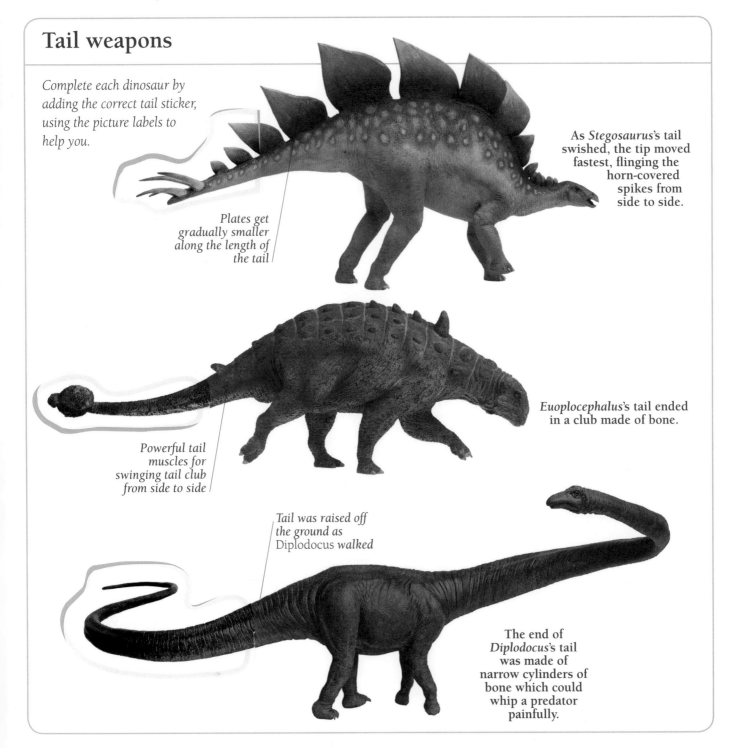

Complete each dinosaur by adding the correct tail sticker, using the picture labels to help you.

As *Stegosaurus's* tail swished, the tip moved fastest, flinging the horn-covered spikes from side to side.

Plates get gradually smaller along the length of the tail

Euoplocephalus's tail ended in a club made of bone.

Powerful tail muscles for swinging tail club from side to side

Tail was raised off the ground as Diplodocus *walked*

The end of *Diplodocus's* tail was made of narrow cylinders of bone which could whip a predator painfully.

Dinosaur calls

Males had longer crests than females

Parasaurolophus

The long, hollow crest on the skull of Parasaurolophus was probably used to make a noise which may have sounded a warning or called the herd together. Scientists do not know exactly what sort of sound Parasaurolophus would have made. Try making a similar resonating sound yourself.

1 Find a long cardboard or plastic tube such as the inside of a roll of foil.

2 Make different sounds through the tube to see what effects you can get. Try blowing or singing sounds such as 'ooo' or 'ah'. Which do you think would be a good dinosaur call?

Peculiar heads

Draw a line to match each caption to the correct picture.

a.

b.

c.

1. To win a mate, a male *Pachycephalosaurus* may have challenged other males by head-butting them with the dome of solid bone on its skull, as stags battle today.

2. The plate-shaped head crests of male *Corythosaurus* were larger than those of females, so they may have been used to attract females in the mating season.

3. *Pentaceratops'* 1 m- (3 ft-) wide neck frill had a hollow framework of bone with skin stretched across the space, making it useless for defence but impressive to mates.

True or false?

Read the following statements about dinosaur defence. Use the information on these two pages and on page 10 to work out which statements are true and which are false, and then tick the correct boxes.

	TRUE	FALSE
1. Dinosaurs with horns are called hadrosaurs.	☐	☐
2. Armoured dinosaurs sometimes crouched to protect their bellies when attacked.	☐	☐
3. Dinosaur spikes were made from hardened skin.	☐	☐
4. *Stegosaurus* had spikes on its back.	☐	☐
5. Horned and armoured dinosaurs walked on four legs.	☐	☐
6. *Parasaurolophus* may have used its hollow crest to sound a warning to the rest of its herd.	☐	☐

Land of the dinosaurs

Throughout most of the Mesozoic, the landscape looked unlike today's world. The climate was much hotter and the flowering plants that form most of Earth's vegetation today did not exist until the Cretaceous. Fronds of ferns and jointed, feathery horsetails covered the ground. The trees were conifers, tree-ferns, and cycads.

Did you know?

Some plants which flourished during the Mesozoic still exist today, such as the Gingko tree which evolved during the Triassic.

Jurassic landscape

Put a letter by each caption to match the correct part of the scene.

1. Large predators such as *Allosaurus*, lurked near the water's edge ready to attack smaller dinosaurs.

2. During the Jurassic, conifers, gingkos, and tree ferns grew into extensive forests, providing food and shelter.

3. Large herbivores such as *Apatosaurus* grazed in herds.

4. Plenty of rain fell to fill lakes and rivers and enable lush vegetation to grow.

5. Smaller dinosaurs, such as *Dryosaurus*, kept watch for large predators.

6. Other animals that existed during the Jurassic included insects, fish, frogs, turtles, crocodile-like reptiles, ichthyosaurs in the oceans and pterosaurs in the skies, as well as the first birds and small mammals.

Use these picture stickers to complete your Activity pages. Place the gold stars on your Progress chart once you have completed each topic and checked your answers.

Coelophysis

Seismosaurus

Euoplocephalus tail

Young adult female
Protoceratops

Triassic Earth

Chinese dragon

Othniel Charles Marsh and
Edward Drinker Cope

Iguanodon tooth

Mature adult female
Protoceratops

Stegosaurus

Newly hatched
Protoceratops

Plateosaurus

Corythosaurus

Carnotaurus

Diplodocus tail

Cretaceous Earth

William Buckland

Tyrannosaurus

Stegosaurus tail

Jurassic Earth

Cold blood or warm blood?

Some scientists think that some dinosaurs were warm-blooded and others were cold-blooded. Use the information in the fact box to work out which group these dinosaurs belong to and write their names in the correct circle.

- **Compsognathus** was an active and intelligent carnivore.

- **Stegosaurus** probably warmed itself by turning its plates towards the sun.

- **Brachiosaurus** was slow-moving and had a very small brain.

- **Velociraptor** had insulating feathers which kept its body warm even at night.

Plates run along the line of Stegosaurus's spine

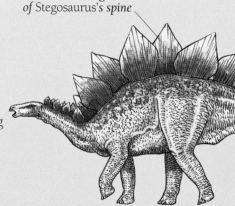

Stegosaurus

warm blood

1....................................

2....................................

cold blood

1....................................

2....................................

Blood facts

- Warm-blooded animals such as birds and mammals convert food energy into body heat.

- Warm-blooded animals have larger brains and more active lifestyles than cold-blooded animals.

- The temperature of cold-blooded animals such as modern reptiles depends on the temperature of their environment.

- Cold-blooded animals spend hours each day basking in the sun to warm their bodies and cannot operate at night or in the cold.

Warm-blooded bird

Cold-blooded snake

Climate puzzle

Add the correct words to complete these statements about the Mesozoic climate. Use the information on these two pages and on page 7 to help you. Choose from:

continents   Cretaceous   dry   horsetails   hotter   rainfall

1. During the Mesozoic it was .... than it is today.

2. The first flowering plants appeared in the ....

3. Earth was warm and .... during the Triassic.

4. There was more .... during the Jurassic than during the Triassic.

5. Earth's climate changed as the .... moved.

6. During the Jurassic, the ground was covered with ferns and .... instead of grass.

Hunting and scavenging

Carnivorous dinosaurs lived in a similar way to lions, gorging themselves with meat after a kill, then resting for days until they grew hungry. The largest carnivores hunted alone, while some smaller carnivores hunted in packs. Some carnivores were scavengers, feeding off animals that had died naturally or scraps left by hunters.

Did you know?

Some carnivores had forward-facing eyes, like modern predators. Each eye gives a slightly different view, which the brain combines to give a 3D image. This allows the animal to judge distances accurately.

Find the sticker

Add the correct sticker to each list of facts comparing lone and pack hunters.

Tyrannosaurus – lone hunter

- Lived alone
- Slow
- Too large to be agile
- Immensely strong
- Attacked where there was plenty of cover for an ambush

Coelophysis – pack hunter

- Lived and hunted in a pack
- Quick
- Very agile
- Not strong individually, but as a pack could hunt very large prey
- Probably attacked by chasing and surrounding prey in the open

Dinosaur battle

Draw lines to link each label to the correct part of the picture.

The **adult *Barosaurus*** rears up to defend its young from an attacking *Allosaurus*.

Barosaurus may try to crush the attacker beneath its **front legs**.

The *Barosaurus* raises its **whip-like tail** ready to launch a stinging blow at the *Allosaurus*.

An ***Allosaurus*** approaches with its jaws open to bite.

The **young *Barosaurus*** hides behind its parent's huge body.

Grazing dinosaurs

Most herbivores lived in large herds, in a similar way to today's grazing animals such as elephants. They would have spent almost every waking hour grazing. If one animal noticed a predator approaching, it may have alerted the rest of the herd with a call. Then the entire herd might stampede at speed away from the attacker.

> ### Did you know?
> Most herbivores had eyes on the sides of their heads giving them good all-round vision so they could watch for predators as they grazed.

Processing food

Number each picture to match the correct sentence below.

a. b. c. d.

1. Duck-billed dinosaurs like this *Lambeosaurus* had flat, toothless beaks at the front of their mouths and small, closely packed teeth at the back.

2. Some herbivores swallowed food without chewing, and then swallowed small stones called gastroliths which ground the food up to help digest it.

3. The *Echinodon's* tiny spiky teeth may have been used to eat animals as well as plants.

4. *Heterodontosaurus* had three types of teeth: sharp beak-like front teeth to snip vegetation, four tusk-like teeth to defend against predators, and ridged cheek teeth to grind up food.

Herbivore puzzle

Circle the correct word to complete each sentence about herbivores.
Use the information on this page and on page 9 to help you.

1. Large herbivores ate **all the time / every few days** to fuel their vast bodies.

2. **Spoon-shaped / peg-like / flat** teeth were used to rake in vegetation.

3. Herbivores that had **cheeks / tusks / gastroliths** were able to keep food in their mouths as they chewed.

4. Hadrosaurs are also known as **omnivorous / horned / duck-billed dinosaurs**.

5. A gastrolith is **a tooth / a stone / an internal organ** that helped some herbivores digest their food.

6. Horned dinosaurs had a **beak / tusk / claw** for snapping off tough vegetation.

Birth and growth

Hatchlings (newly hatched dinosaurs) grew very quickly for the first few months. For the next six years, juveniles (young dinosaurs) continued to grow fast. Different species reached adult size and shape in different lengths of time. For example, *Tyrannosaurus* was fully grown at about 20 while *Maiasaura* was adult at eight.

Did you know?

Between the ages of 15 and 20, *Tyrannosaurus* had a growth spurt when it put on more than 2 kg (4.4 lb) per day.

Parental care

Match each label to the correct box on the picture and write in the number.

Maiasaura family

1. *Maiasaura* nests were up to 1 m (3 ft) high.
2. New hatchlings were about 30 cm (12 in) long.
3. At one year old, *Maiasaura* had grown to around 3 m (10 ft).
4. Parents continued to feed their young until they could fend for themselves.
5. An adult *Maiasaura* could reach 9 m (27 ft) tall.

Growing up

Add three stickers to show how the skull of Protoceratops changed as the dinosaur grew.

Frill extends

Beak

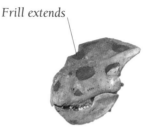

Newly hatched *Protoceratops* had a very small beak and head frill.

The beak became more distinctive in babies.

The frill at the back of the skull began to grow wider as *Protoceratops* grew larger.

In young adult females, the frill was not much wider than the skull.

Bone of frill develops

Frill

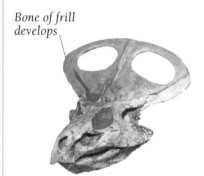

Cheek bones

Beak

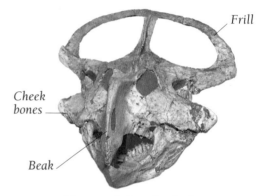

Young adult males had a wider skull frill.

Mature adult females had a narrow, beak-like snout and wide cheek bones.

Mature adult males had a beak, large cheek bones and a wide frill.

Eggs and nests

Add the correct words to complete these statements about dinosaur nests and eggs. Use the information on these two pages and on page 11 to help you. Choose from:

brittle   crushed   earth   incubate   migrated   newly hatched

1. Some dinosaurs .... to the same nesting site year after year.

2. Some dinosaurs made a nest by scraping up a mound of.....................

3. Dinosaur eggs were hard and ....

4. Mother dinosaurs may have used body heat to .... the eggs until they hatched.

5. *Maiasaura* were about 30 cm (12 in) when they were ....

6. When dinosaurs stayed in the nest for a long time after hatching, ... eggshell is found in the nest.

***Maiasaura* emerging from its egg**

Nest facts

- Some dinosaurs, such as *Maiasaura*, lined their nests with leaves and twigs.

- Some scraped a nest from a mound of earth to stop the eggs rolling away.

- Not all the eggs in a nest hatched at the same time.

- Some dinosaurs had a seasonal migration, moving to good grazing areas for part of the year and travelling back to the same nesting site each year to lay their eggs in a huge colony with other members of the same species.

Other prehistoric creatures

During the Mesozoic, dinosaurs were not the only large reptiles that existed. The air was filled with flying reptiles called pterosaurs. The smallest were the size of sparrows, while the largest were the size of a small aeroplane. In the oceans, there were many families of marine reptiles, including ichthyosaurs and pliosaurs. These reptiles lived underwater but had to return to the surface to breathe, as dolphins do today.

Did you know?

The largest pterosaur, *Quetzalcoatlus*, had a wing-span of 11 m (36 ft), about the same as the wingspan of a World War II Spitfire aircraft.

Find the dinosaurs

Read the information around these prehistoric animals, looking out for the clues that will tell you whether they are dinosaurs or not.

Use the dinosaur definition panel on page 31 to help you. Then tick one box under each picture.

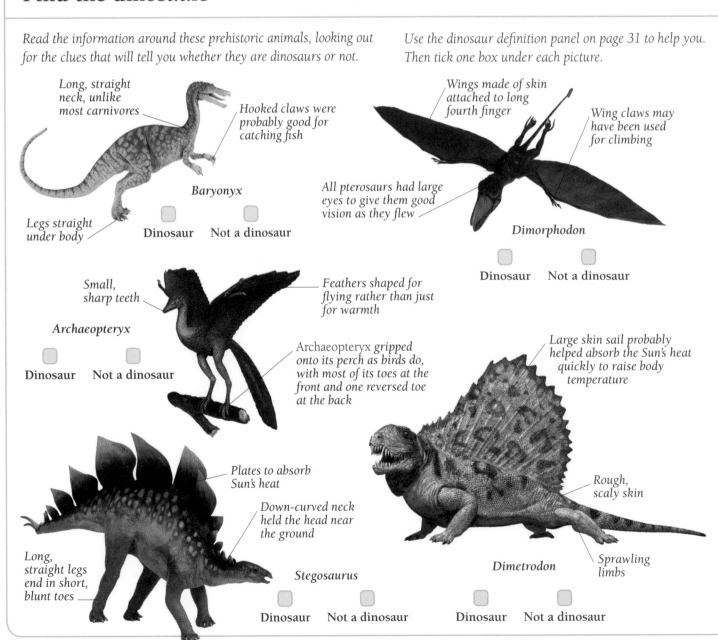

Long, straight neck, unlike most carnivores

Hooked claws were probably good for catching fish

Baryonyx

Legs straight under body

☐ Dinosaur ☐ Not a dinosaur

Wings made of skin attached to long fourth finger

Wing claws may have been used for climbing

All pterosaurs had large eyes to give them good vision as they flew

Dimorphodon

☐ Dinosaur ☐ Not a dinosaur

Small, sharp teeth

Feathers shaped for flying rather than just for warmth

Archaeopteryx

☐ Dinosaur ☐ Not a dinosaur

Archaeopteryx gripped onto its perch as birds do, with most of its toes at the front and one reversed toe at the back

Large skin sail probably helped absorb the Sun's heat quickly to raise body temperature

Plates to absorb Sun's heat

Down-curved neck held the head near the ground

Rough, scaly skin

Long, straight legs end in short, blunt toes

Stegosaurus

Dimetrodon

Sprawling limbs

☐ Dinosaur ☐ Not a dinosaur ☐ Dinosaur ☐ Not a dinosaur

Dinosaur definition

Use the information on page 6 to help you answer the following questions.

	YES	NO			YES	NO
1. Were dinosaurs reptiles?	☐	☐	6. Did any dinosaurs have feathers?		☐	☐
2. Were dinosaurs mammals?	☐	☐	7. Did dinosaurs lay eggs?		☐	☐
3. Did dinosaurs live in the water?	☐	☐	8. Did dinosaurs give birth to live young?		☐	☐
4. Did dinosaurs live on land?	☐	☐	9. Did dinosaurs have sprawling legs?		☐	☐
5. Could dinosaurs fly?	☐	☐	10. Did dinosaurs have straight legs?		☐	☐

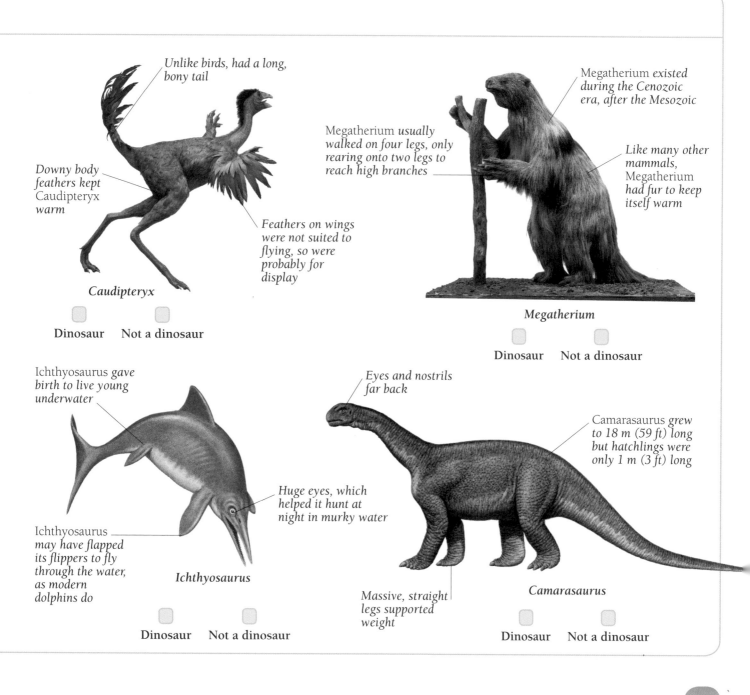

Unlike birds, had a long, bony tail

Downy body feathers kept Caudipteryx warm

Feathers on wings were not suited to flying, so were probably for display

Caudipteryx

☐ ☐
Dinosaur   Not a dinosaur

Megatherium existed during the Cenozoic era, after the Mesozoic

Megatherium usually walked on four legs, only rearing onto two legs to reach high branches

Like many other mammals, Megatherium had fur to keep itself warm

Megatherium

☐ ☐
Dinosaur   Not a dinosaur

Ichthyosaurus gave birth to live young underwater

Huge eyes, which helped it hunt at night in murky water

Ichthyosaurus may have flapped its flippers to fly through the water, as modern dolphins do

Ichthyosaurus

☐ ☐
Dinosaur   Not a dinosaur

Eyes and nostrils far back

Camarasaurus grew to 18 m (59 ft) long but hatchlings were only 1 m (3 ft) long

Massive, straight legs supported weight

Camarasaurus

☐ ☐
Dinosaur   Not a dinosaur

Dinosaur discoveries

Some dinosaur fossils are discovered by chance, by people mining or quarrying underground. But most new fossil finds are discovered on Earth's surface, exposed when areas of land shift or become eroded (worn away by weather). In the past, people thought these massive bones might be the bones of giants or mythical beasts.

Dinosaur hunting

Use your back-cover chart to fill in the missing information about the first dinosaur hunters and early dinosaur discoveries. Then find four stickers to put in the missing picture spaces.

1. In ancient China, people believed that dinosaur bones were the remains of dead dragons.

2. Dr Gideon Mantell and his wife Mary Ann found teeth and bones in a quarry in the year .... Dr Mantell worked out that the remains belonged to a giant reptile which he named *Iguanodon*.

3. Dr William Buckland published a description of an animal called *Megalosaurus* in 1824. Although this was before the word 'dinosaur' had been invented, it was the first scientific description of a dinosaur.

4. American fossil hunters O.C. Marsh and Edward Drinker Cope were rivals in the race to find new dinosaurs. In the late 1880s they identified almost 130 new species.

5. Famous American dinosaur hunter Barnum Brown was the first to find *Tyrannosaurus*, between .... and .... in the Red Deer River Valley in Alberta, Canada.

6. American Roy Chapman Andrews discovered the first .... and hatchlings in the Gobi Desert between 1922 and 1925.

Mud excavation

When a new fossil is found, explosives or bulldozers remove large sections of rock covering the find. The fossil, along with some of the surrounding rock, is removed with chisels. The fossil is carefully wrapped for transportation to the laboratory, where the remaining rock is removed and the fossil is cleaned using chemicals or fine tools.

Now try digging for fossils yourself by making a fossil mud pie. You will need: • large, old plastic container • soil • water • hard, dead objects to bury, such as bones, shells, seeds, coins, small toys • trowel • paintbrush • toothpick • tweezers

1 Half-fill the plastic container with soil. Break it up with your hands until it is as fine as possible.

2 Pour in water and mix with your hands until it is sticky but not runny.

3 Push the objects into the mud. Leave the container in a dry place for several days until the mud has set hard.

4 Tip out the mud-pie outside. Carefully excavate the objects. Use a trowel to dig away large pieces of mud, a paintbrush to brush soil away gently, and tweezers and a toothpick to remove small, delicate items.

Fossils

Bones are porous, which means that they are full of tiny holes like a sponge. When bone fossilizes, water containing minerals soaks into these holes from the mud or sand around the bone. Gradually the bone is dissolved by the minerals, and the minerals harden into rock, forming a fossil cast or replica of the bone.

Did you know?

Finding an entire fossil skeleton happens very rarely. Usually the skeleton is incomplete because part of it has been washed away by rivers or seas, or because the animal's corpse was torn apart by scavengers after its death.

How fossils are formed

Add the correct words to complete this step-by-step explanation of how dinosaurs turn into fossils. Use the information on this page and on page 12 to help you. Choose from:

erosion   minerals   scavengers   soft

1. The body of a dead dinosaur is buried in the soft mud at the edge of a river or ocean, which protects it from ....

2. The .... parts of the dead dinosaur rot away underground, leaving just the skeleton.

3. Over thousands of years, ... soak into the skeleton, and the bones and teeth turn into fossils.

4. Millions of years later, ground movements or .... expose the bones of the fossilized dinosaur.

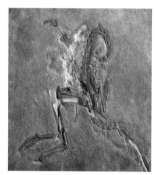

Fossilized *Compsognathus* still embedded in rock

Make a fossil bone

 WARNING Always wear gloves and goggles whenever you handle the Epsom salts.

Investigate how fossilization works by making a fake fossil.

1 Draw a bone shape on the sponge, then cut it out with scissors.

2 With the help of an adult, put two thirds of a cup of Epsom salts into a jug, then add half a cup of hot water. Stir with a spoon until the salt dissolves.

You will need:
- *synthetic bath sponge • felt-tip pen*
- *scissors • protective gloves and goggles*
- *Epsom salts • jug • measuring cup*
- *hot water • spoon • plastic container a little bigger than the sponge*

3 Place the bone in the plastic container and pour in enough Epsom salt solution to cover about a third of the bone.

4 Turn the sponge over every day until most of the solution has dried up. What does it feel like? Look at page 45 to find out why.

How to rebuild a dinosaur

Working out what a dinosaur looked like and how it lived takes complex detective work. Once the skeleton is reconstructed, muscle attachment points on bones show the size and shape of muscles, helping to reconstruct the body shape. A dinosaur's posture and way of moving can be recreated based on its muscles and footprints.

Rebuilding *Barosaurus*

Most excavated fossils are too delicate to go on display in a museum, so reproductions are made of them. Read the captions below and look at the pictures. Number them 1 to 6 to show how a reproduction Barosaurus was put on display.

The mould is peeled away from the bone, then resin, plastic, or plaster of Paris is poured into it to form a **cast of the bone**.

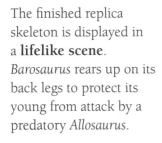

The finished replica skeleton is displayed in a **lifelike scene**. *Barosaurus* rears up on its back legs to protect its young from attack by a predatory *Allosaurus*.

First the fossilized dinosaur bones are painted with rubber to make a **flexible mould**.

The skeleton is rebuilt from the bottom up. The **highest pieces** have to be winched into place using mobile lifting platforms.

Each replica bone is drilled so a metal rod can run through it. The **rods are welded** together to join the bones.

The cast is removed from the mould, then a **modeller smoothes the rough edges** of the replica bone.

Fossil impression

Some fossils are replicas of impressions left behind by things that were once living, which then filled up with minerals which hardened into rock over time. Fossil impressions can preserve dinosaur footprints or delicate feathers or plants. See how this works by making a fake impression fossil.

1 Make a thick flattened disc with modelling clay.

2 Press an object into the modelling clay. Remove it, taking care not to damage the impression you have made.

3 Cut a card strip and press it into the modelling clay to form a circle around the impression.

4 Mix some plaster of Paris following the instructions on the packet. Add a little yellow food colouring and sand to the plaster if you want your fake fossil to look like rock.

5 When the plaster begins to thicken, pour a 1 cm (0.5 in) layer into the card circle.

6 Leave for a day to set, then remove the card and peel off the clay to see your fake fossil.

Monster mistakes

Sometimes scientists make mistakes when they reconstruct dinosaurs, or their ideas are proved wrong by later discoveries. Read each caption, then write the letter of the picture it describes in the box.

1. Films and cartoons sometimes portray early people battling with dinosaurs, but in fact dinosaurs had been extinct for 64 million years before the first humans evolved.

a.

2. When *Hypsilophodon* fossils were first discovered, scientists believed that these small herbivores lived in the trees. Now scientists have shown that *Hypsilophodon* was a small, agile, ground-dwelling dinosaur.

b.

3. Some people claim that the mysterious long-necked monster that is said to dwell in Scotland's Loch Ness is an ancient marine reptile such as *Elasmosaurus* that survived the Cretaceous extinction.

c.

4. When scientists discovered a small carnivore near a nest of what they thought were *Protoceratops* eggs, they named it *Oviraptor*, or 'egg-thief'. It was later discovered that the nest actually contained *Oviraptor*'s own eggs. It was guarding its eggs, not stealing someone else's!

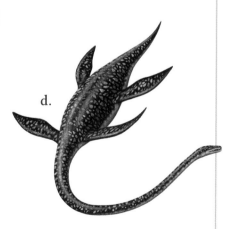

d.

From dinosaur to bird

Some dinosaurs, such as *Sinosauropteryx*, were covered with soft down which kept them warm. Some later dinosaurs, such as *Caudipteryx*, had longer clumps of feathers, which may have been for display. The discovery of dinosaurs with feathers suggests that birds are the living descendants of dinosaurs.

Did you know?

Surprisingly, birds did not evolve from bird-hipped ornithischian dinosaurs but from lizard-hipped saurischians. Many small carnivores have skeletons that are almost identical to the earliest birds.

Deinonychus, a small Cretaceous carnivore

How birds evolved

Circle the correct word to complete each sentence about the evolution of birds. Use the information on this page and on page 13 to help you.

1. The small dinosaurs that evolved into birds were **carnivores / herbivores**.

2. The first known bird is called *Caudipteryx / Velociraptor / Archaeopteryx*.

3. *Archaeopteryx* lived **before / during / after** the Mesozoic era.

4. Some dinosaurs had **fur / downy feathers** to keep themselves warm.

5. Early birds had **a long, bony / a short, stumpy / no tail**.

6. The first birds had **claws / teeth / wishbones** on the front of their wings.

Feather facts

- Feathers used for flying have off-centre shafts. Birds that can fly have these feathers, but dinosaurs did not have them.

Off-centre shaft

Flight feathers

- Feathers with central shafts cannot be used for flight. These feathers are found on dinosaurs and birds.

Central shaft **Display feathers**

- Soft down feathers keep the body warm. These feathers are found on dinosaurs and birds.

Fluffy texture **Down feather**

The first bird

The earliest birds, such as Archaeopteryx had developed some bird features, such as a wishbone across the chest, while still retaining some reptile features. Draw a line to link each label to the correct dot on the picture.

1. Clawed fingers set at front of wings, unlike a modern bird

2. Teeth, like a reptile but unlike a modern bird

3. Long, bony tail, like a reptile but unlike a modern bird

4. Long flight feathers, like a bird

5. Reversible toe for perching, like a bird

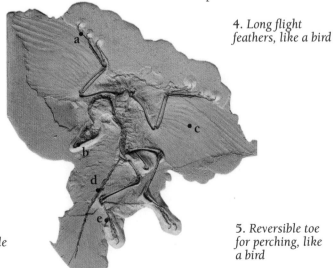

Archaeopteryx fossil

End of the dinosaur age

Sixty-five million years ago, around 50 per cent of all species of animal on Earth became extinct, including all the dinosaurs. By the end of the Cretaceous, there were no land animals left that were bigger than a dog. Most scientists believe that this mass extinction was caused by the impact of a massive meteorite hitting Earth.

After the impact

Add arrows from one shape to another, to show what may have happened step by step after a meteor impact. Use the information on this page and on page 13 to help you.

A huge meteorite fell to Earth from space.

As the herbivores died out, the carnivores were left with no food source, so they died.

With no plants to eat, herbivores died.

Lack of sunlight killed off green plants.

The impact of the meteorite caused a huge cloud of dust to block out the Sun's light, making the planet cold and dark for years.

Survivors facts

- One theory about why some creatures survived while others did not is that all the survivors were small active scavengers which were able to find food from a range of sources, such as dead animals and rotting vegetation.

- During the Mesozoic, all the mammals that existed were very small. Larger ones, such as the woolly mammoth, began to evolve once the dinosaurs were extinct.

Woolly mammoth

True or false?

Read the following statements about the extinction of the dinosaurs. Use the information on this page and on page 13 to work out which statements are true and which are false, and then tick the correct box.

	TRUE	FALSE
1. The dinosaurs all died out 248 million years ago.	☐	☐
2. All flying reptiles became extinct at the same time as the dinosaurs.	☐	☐
3. A meteorite is a rock that falls to Earth from space.	☐	☐
4. Scientists think that the extinction may have been caused by a massive meteorite impact off the coast of Mexico.	☐	☐
5. Animals that survived the extinction may have fed off the dead animals and vegetation.	☐	☐
6. Large mammals existed at the same time as the dinosaurs.	☐	☐

Dinosaur bodies

Tick or number the boxes to answer each question. Check your answers on page 46

1 Which group do dinosaurs *not* belong to?

- ☐ a. mammals
- ☐ b. archosaurs
- ☐ c. animals
- ☐ d. reptiles

2 How many species of dinosaur have been named?

- ☐ a. 70
- ☐ b. 700
- ☐ c. 7000
- ☐ d. 70,000

3 The two groups of dinosaurs, ornithschian and saurischian, are divided according to the shape of their:

- ☐ a. skulls
- ☐ b. teeth
- ☐ c. backbones
- ☐ d. hips

4 In what way were dinosaurs similar to mammals?

- ☐ a. They gave birth to live young.
- ☐ b. They had straight legs tucked under their bodies.
- ☐ c. They fed their young on milk.

5 The smallest dinosaurs were the size of:

- ☐ a. a blue whale
- ☐ b. a dog
- ☐ c. a grasshopper
- ☐ d. a chicken

6 The largest dinosaurs weighed the same as how many African elephants?

- ☐ a. 2
- ☐ b. 5
- ☐ c. 10
- ☐ d. 12

7 Number these dinosaurs 1 to 4 from smallest to biggest:

- ☐ a. *Velociraptor*
- ☐ b. *Brachiosaurus*
- ☐ c. *Triceratops*
- ☐ d. *Allosaurus*

8 Tick all the facts that are true about carnivores:

- ☐ a. They ate meat.
- ☐ b. They walked on four legs.
- ☐ c. They did not chew.
- ☐ d. Their teeth often curved backwards.

9 Tick one thing *Iguanodon* did not have on its hands:

- ☐ a. fang
- ☐ b. hoof
- ☐ c. thumb spike
- ☐ d. flexible finger

10 Which dinosaur had the smallest brain compared to its body size?

- ☐ a. *Compsognathus*
- ☐ b. *Apatosaurus*
- ☐ c. *Iguanodon*
- ☐ d. *Stegosaurus*

11 Scientists don't know what colour dinosaurs were because:

- ☐ a. no dinosaur skin has ever been found
- ☐ b. skin loses its colour when it is fossilized
- ☐ c. dinosaur fossils are all covered with mud
- ☐ d. dinosaurs were invisible

Mesozoic world

Tick or number the boxes to answer each question. Check your answers on page 46

1 Dinosaurs existed on the Earth for:

☐ **a.** 150,000 years
☐ **b.** 1.5 million years
☐ **c.** 15 million years
☐ **d.** 150 million years

2 Number these periods of the Mesozoic era 1 to 3 to show the order they happened.

☐ **a.** Jurassic
☐ **b.** Triassic
☐ **c.** Cretaceous

3 Pangea was:

☐ **a.** a Triassic supercontinent
☐ **b.** a Triassic plant
☐ **c.** a Triassic carnivore
☐ **d.** a Triassic pterosaur

4 Tick all the plants that grew during the Jurassic:

☐ **a.** ferns
☐ **b.** daffodils
☐ **c.** horsetails
☐ **d.** conifers

5 The first flowering plants appeared during the:

☐ **a.** Cretaceous
☐ **b.** Jurassic
☐ **c.** Paleaozoic
☐ **d.** Triassic

6 Tick all the places where dinosaurs did *not* live:

☐ **a.** in the sea
☐ **b.** on the land
☐ **c.** in the skies

7 Which animal did *not* exist at the same time as the dinosaurs?

☐ **a.** lizard
☐ **b.** pterosaur
☐ **c.** turtle
☐ **d.** human

8 Tick all the creatures that lived in the sea during the Mesozoic.

☐ **a.** pliosaurs
☐ **b.** ichthyosaurs
☐ **c.** pterosaurs
☐ **d.** hadrosaurs

9 How did *Ichthyosaurus* give birth?

☐ **a.** It laid eggs on land.
☐ **b.** It laid eggs in the water.
☐ **c.** It gave birth to live young in the water.
☐ **d.** It gave birth to live young on land.

10 How big was the wingspan of *Quetzalcoatlus*?

☐ **a.** 1 m (3 feet)
☐ **b.** 11 m (36 feet)
☐ **c.** 21 m (70 feet)
☐ **d.** 31 m (100 ft)

11 What were pterosaurs' wings made from?

☐ **a.** feathers
☐ **b.** scales
☐ **c.** skin
☐ **d.** fur

Attack and defence

Tick or number the boxes to answer each question. Check your answers on page 46

1 To protect their soft stomachs, armoured dinosaurs sometimes:

- ☐ **a.** rolled up in a ball
- ☐ **b.** crouched on the ground
- ☐ **c.** turned over on their backs
- ☐ **d.** covered them with their tails

2 Which group of dinosaurs did horned dinosaurs belong to?

- ☐ **a.** anklyosaurs
- ☐ **b.** ceratopsians
- ☐ **c.** pterosaurs
- ☐ **d.** theropods

3 Flat, bony plates in dinosaur skin are called:

- ☐ **a.** horns
- ☐ **b.** platters
- ☐ **c.** scutes
- ☐ **d.** shells

4 What did *Euoplocephalus* have on the end of its tail?

- ☐ **a.** a spike
- ☐ **b.** a club
- ☐ **c.** a whip
- ☐ **d.** a horn

5 Dinosaur spikes were made from:

- ☐ **a.** bone and horn
- ☐ **b.** toughened hair
- ☐ **c.** toughened skin
- ☐ **d.** bone and skin

6 Tick all the ways carnivorous dinosaurs hunted their prey.

- ☐ **a.** They crept up and attacked their prey with a sudden charge.
- ☐ **b.** They chased their prey at great speed.
- ☐ **c.** They swooped down on their prey from the sky.
- ☐ **d.** They surrounded their prey in a pack.

7 How did a male *Pachycephalosaurus* fight other males in the mating season?

- ☐ **a.** by slashing them with its long, sharp horns
- ☐ **b.** by punching them with its strong forelimbs
- ☐ **c.** by whipping them with its spiky tail
- ☐ **d.** by butting them with the dome of solid bone of its head

8 Where did *Tyrannosaurus* hunt?

- ☐ **a.** in the open
- ☐ **b.** at the edge of the ocean
- ☐ **c.** in places where there was plenty of vegetation
- ☐ **d.** in the desert

9 It is useful for a hunter to have forward-facing eyes because it helps them to:

- ☐ **a.** see all around themselves
- ☐ **b.** judge distances
- ☐ **c.** see things that are far away
- ☐ **d.** see things that are very small

Dinosaur lives

Tick or number the boxes to answer each question. Check your answers on page 46

1 Dinosaur eggs were:

- ☐ **a.** hard and brittle
- ☐ **b.** jelly-like
- ☐ **c.** soft and leathery
- ☐ **d.** solid like a rock

2 How big were the largest dinosaur eggs?

- ☐ **a.** 30 cm (1 ft)
- ☐ **b.** 60 cm (2 ft)
- ☐ **c.** 90 cm (3 ft)
- ☐ **d.** 1.2 m (4 ft)

3 Dinosaur laid their eggs:

- ☐ **a.** in water
- ☐ **b.** in nests in trees
- ☐ **c.** in nests scraped in the ground
- ☐ **d.** in caves

4 Which dinosaurs were the most intelligent?

- ☐ **a.** carnivores that lived in a pack
- ☐ **b.** herbivores that lived in a herd
- ☐ **c.** carnivores that lived alone
- ☐ **d.** herbivores that lived alone

5 Tick all the reasons why fast-moving carnivores may have been warm-blooded.

- ☐ **a.** They sweated a lot.
- ☐ **b.** They were very active.
- ☐ **c.** They had sharp claws.
- ☐ **d.** They were intelligent.

6 How fast could the fastest dinosaurs run?

- ☐ **a.** 8 kph (5 mph)
- ☐ **b.** 16 kph (10 mph)
- ☐ **c.** 80 kph (50 mph)
- ☐ **d.** 160 kph (100 mph)

7 What is a scavenger?

- ☐ **a.** an animal that feeds off animals that are already dead
- ☐ **b.** an animal that kills prey and eats it
- ☐ **c.** an animal that eats only fish
- ☐ **d.** an animal that eats only eggs

8 Herbivores spent most of the day:

- ☐ **a.** hunting
- ☐ **b.** sleeping
- ☐ **c.** eating
- ☐ **d.** walking

9 To help them digest food, some herbivores swallowed stones called:

- ☐ **a.** coprolites
- ☐ **b.** hadrosaurs
- ☐ **c.** scutes
- ☐ **d.** gastroliths

10 Which one of these is *not* a herbivore?

- ☐ **a.** *Triceratops*
- ☐ **b.** *Plateosaurus*
- ☐ **c.** *Allosaurus*
- ☐ **d.** *Corythosaurus*

11 *Pentaceratops* had a 1-m (3-ft)wide:

- ☐ **a.** head spike
- ☐ **b.** neck frill
- ☐ **c.** tail club
- ☐ **d.** beak

Fossil finding

Tick or number the boxes to answer each question. Check your answers on page 46

1 Palaeontology is the study of:

- ☐ **a.** dinosaurs
- ☐ **b.** fossils
- ☐ **c.** rocks
- ☐ **d.** the past

2 Fossils are made of:

- ☐ **a.** bone
- ☐ **b.** rock
- ☐ **c.** water
- ☐ **d.** mud

3 Tick all the things that may be preserved as fossils:

- ☐ **a.** bones
- ☐ **b.** footprints
- ☐ **c.** feathers
- ☐ **d.** skin colour
- ☐ **e.** teeth

4 Number the stages 1 to 4 to show how a fossil is formed.

- ☐ **a.** The minerals gradually replace the bone.
- ☐ **b.** Soft parts of the body rot away.
- ☐ **c.** Dinosaur is buried in mud.
- ☐ **d.** Water seeps through the bones, leaving behind minerals.

5 What is a coprolite?

- ☐ **a.** fossilized dinosaur dung
- ☐ **b.** a fossilized mushroom
- ☐ **c.** a fossilized dinosaur nest
- ☐ **d.** a fossilized dinosaur brain

6 Minerals can soak into bones to form fossils because:

- ☐ **a.** bones are porous
- ☐ **b.** bones are soft
- ☐ **c.** bones are hard
- ☐ **d.** bones are brittle

7 Tick all the places where fossil are often found.

- ☐ **a.** in mines
- ☐ **b.** in quarries
- ☐ **c.** in fields
- ☐ **d.** under the sea

8 Number these palaeontologists 1 to 5 from earliest to latest in order of their famous discoveries:

- ☐ **a.** Barnum Brown
- ☐ **b.** Luis Chiappe
- ☐ **c.** Gideon Mantell
- ☐ **d.** O.C. Marsh and Edward Drinker Cope
- ☐ **e.** Paul Sereno

9 Tick one item which is *not* needed when making a dinosaur reproduction.

- ☐ **a.** metal rods
- ☐ **b.** rock
- ☐ **c.** rubber
- ☐ **d.** plaster of Paris

10 What did Roy Chapman Andrews find in the Gobi Desert?

- ☐ **a.** *Tyrannosaurus*
- ☐ **b.** *Iguanodon*
- ☐ **c.** dinosaur nests
- ☐ **d.** feathered dinosaurs

Dinosaur destruction

Tick or number the boxes to answer each question. Check your answers on page 46

1 Dinosaurs became extinct:

☐ **a.** 230 million years ago
☐ **b.** 195 million years ago
☐ **c.** 141 million years ago
☐ **d.** 65 million years ago

2 Tick all the animals that did *not* become extinct at the same time as the dinosaurs:

☐ **a.** mammals
☐ **b.** birds
☐ **c.** pterosaurs
☐ **d.** amphibians

3 Number the sequence 1 to 6 to show what happened when the dinosaurs became extinct.

☐ **a.** Animals that fed on plants died.
☐ **b.** The dust blocked out the Sun's light.
☐ **c.** A massive meteor fell to Earth.
☐ **d.** Carnivores had no prey, so they died.
☐ **e.** With no light plants died.
☐ **f.** A cloud of dust was thrown into the atmosphere.

4 The meteorite fell to Earth off the coast of:

☐ **a.** Mexico
☐ **b.** Japan
☐ **c.** France
☐ **d.** Australia

5 What percentage of all the species of animals on Earth became extinct at the same time as the dinosaurs?

☐ **a.** 20
☐ **b.** 30
☐ **c.** 40
☐ **d.** 50

6 Tick all the things that animals that survived the extinction lived off:

☐ **a.** dead animals
☐ **b.** live prey
☐ **c.** fresh green plants
☐ **d.** rotting vegetation

7 Birds developed from:

☐ **a.** pterosaurs
☐ **b.** small carnivorous dinosaurs
☐ **c.** small herbivorous dinosaurs
☐ **d.** bats

8 Tick all the dinosaurs that had feathers:

☐ **a.** *Sinosauropteryx*
☐ **b.** *Apatosaurus*
☐ **c.** *Caudipteryx*
☐ **d.** *Stegosaurus*

9 The first bird, *Archaeopteryx* lived during the:

☐ **a.** Triassic
☐ **b.** Jurassic
☐ **c.** Cretaceous
☐ **d.** Middle Ages

10 Tick one feature of *Archaeopteryx* which is not found on birds.

☐ **a.** feathers
☐ **b.** teeth
☐ **c.** reversible toe
☐ **d.** wishbone

11 Palaeontologists believe birds evolved from dinosaurs because they have discovered:

☐ **a.** dinosaurs with feathers
☐ **b.** dinosaurs that could fly
☐ **c.** dinosaurs that have beaks
☐ **d.** dinosaurs that can sing

Activity answers

Once you have completed each page of activities, check your answers below.

Page 14
How dinosaurs evolved
a 4
b 3
c 2
d 1

Page 15
Name the dinosaurs

No.	Translation
3	terrible claw
2	parrot lizard
1	three-horned face

Page 15
True or false?
1 False – the two main groups depend on the shape of their hips.
2 True
3 False – they all ate plants.
4 True
5 True
6 False – saurischians had hip bones which pointed in opposite directions.

Pages 16 and 17
Dinosaur times
Triassic period **230–195** mya
The earliest known dinosaur was ***Herrerasaurus***.
Jurassic period **195–141 mya**
Seismosaurus, the largest dinosaur that ever existed
Cretaceous period **141–65 mya**
Giganotosaurus is the biggest carnivore that has ever been discovered.
Cretaceous carnivore **Microraptor** is the smallest dinosaur ever found.

Page 18
Dinosaur differences

	Carnivore	Herbivore
Diet	meat	plants
Teeth	razor-sharp, often curved	peg-like, spoon-shaped, or flat
Jaws	long, with strong muscles	usually light with weaker muscles
Movement	walked or ran on two legs	some on two legs; others on four legs
Triassic example	*Eoraptor*	*Plateosaurus*
Jurassic example	*Allosaurus*	*Brachiosaurus*
Cretaceous example	*Tyrannosaurus*	*Iguanodon*

Page 19
Dinosaur skin
1 pebbly scales
2 covered in patterns
3 feathers
4 flexible armoured plates

Page 19
How big were dinosaurs?
1 *Compsognathus*
2 *Tyrannosaurus*
3 *Brachiosaurus*

Page 20
Walking and grasping
1 Three forward-pointing hoof-like toes
2 Solid, inflexible thumb spike
3 Flexible, jointed fifth finger
4 Strong, broad foot
5 Small first toe
6 Four powerful but inflexible toes

Iguanodon – hand
Scelidosaurus – foot

Page 20
Dinosaur hands
Only your little finger will bend to grasp the objects.

Page 21
Claws
1 knuckles
2 slashing
3 digging
4 curved

Page 21
Movement puzzle
1 carnivores
2 tails
3 *Gallimimus*
4 *Iguanodon*
5 digging

Page 23
Peculiar heads
1 c
2 a
3 b

Page 23
True or false?
1 False – they are called ceratopsians.
2 True
3 False – they were made from bone covered with horn.
4 True
5 True
6 True

Page 24
Jurassic landscape
1 d   4 e
2 a   5 b
3 f   6 c

Page 25
Cold blood or warm blood?
Warm blood: *Compsognathus*, *Velociraptor*
Cold blood: *Stegosaurus*, *Brachiosaurus*

Climate puzzle

1 hotter   4 rainfall
2 Cretaceous   5 continents
3 dry   6 horsetails

Page 26
Dinosaur battle

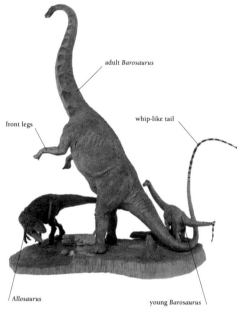

adult *Barosaurus*

whip-like tail

front legs

Allosaurus

young *Barosaurus*

Page 27
Processing food

a 4
b 1
c 2
d 3

Page 27
Herbivore puzzle

1 all the time   4 duck-billed
2 peg-like   5 a stone
3 cheeks   6 beak

Page 28
Parental care

Page 29
Eggs and nests

1 migrated   4 incubate
2 earth   5 newly hatched
3 brittle   6 crushed

Pages 30 and 31
Find the dinosaurs

Dinosaur
Baryonyx
Stegosaurus
Caudipteryx
Camarasaurus

Not a dinosaur
Dimorphodon – flying reptile
Archaeopteryx – bird
Dimetrodon – reptile with sprawling limbs
Megatherium – mammal
Ichthyosaurus – marine reptile

Page 31
Dinosaur definition

1 yes   6 yes
2 no   7 yes
3 no   8 no
4 yes   9 no
5 no   10 yes

Page 32
Dinosaur hunting

2 1822
5 1910 and 1915
6 dinosaur nests

Page 33
Make a fossil bone

The sponge should feel heavier and harder. Crystals of dry Epsom salts have formed in the holes in the sponge, in the way minerals solidify to form fossils. Look at the crystals in your fake fossil bone with a magnifying glass.

Page 33
How fossils are formed

1 scavengers   3 minerals
2 soft   4 erosion

Page 34
Rebuilding *Barosaurus*

1 flexible mould
2 cast of the bone
3 modeller smoothes the rough edges
4 rods are welded
5 highest pieces
6 lifelike scene

Page 35
Monster mistakes

1 b   3 d
2 c   4 a

Page 36
How birds evolved

1 carnivores
2 *Archaeopteryx*
3 during
4 downy feathers
5 long, bony
6 claws

Page 36
The first bird

1 a; 2 b; 3 d; 4 c; 5 e

Page 37
After the meteor impact

- A huge meteorite fell to Earth from space.
- The impact of the meteorite caused a huge cloud of dust to block out the Sun's light, making the planet cold and dark for years.
- Lack of sunlight killed off green plants.
- With no plants to eat, herbivores died.
- As the herbivores died out, the carnivores were left with no food source, so they died.

Answers

Page 37
True or false?
1 False – the dinosaurs died out 65 million years ago.
2 True
3 True
4 True
5 True
6 False – large mammals only evolved after the extinction of the dinosaurs.

Quick quiz answers
Once you have completed each page of quiz questions, check your answers below.

page 38
Dinosaur bodies
1 a 2 b 3 d 4 b 5 d 6 c 7 a 1, b 4, c 2, d 3 8 a c d 9 a 10 d 11 b

page 39
Mesozoic world
1 d 2 a 2, b 1, c 3 3 a 4 a c d 5 a 6 a c 7 d 8 a b 9 c 10 b 11 c

page 40
Attack and defence
1 b 2 b 3 c 4 b 5 a 6 a b d 7 d 8 c 9 b

page 41
Dinosaur lives
1 a 2 b 3 c 4 a 5 b d 6 c 7 a 8 c 9 d 10 c 11 b

page 42
Fossil finding
1 b 2 b 3 a b c e 4 a 4, b 2, c 1, d 3 5 a 6 a 7 a b 8 a 3, b 5, c 1, d 2, e 4 9 b 10 c

page 43
Dinosaur destruction
1 d 2 a b d 3 a 5, b 3, c 1, d 6, e 4, f 2 4 a 5 d 6 a d 7 b 8 a c 9 b 10 b 11 a

Acknowledgements

The publisher would like to thank the following:

Sue Lightfoot and Julie Ferris for proof-reading.

The publisher would like to thank the following for their kind permission to reproduce their photographs:

(Key: a-above; b-below/bottom; c-centre; f-far; l-left; r-right; t-top)

DK Images: 2 Senckenberg, Forschungsinstitut und Naturmuseum, Frankfurt (br). **6** Senckenberg, Forschungsinstitut und Naturmuseum, Frankfurt (cl). **8** Natural History Museum, London (clb); Staatliches Museum für Naturkunde Stuttgart (bc). **9** Natural History Museum, London (clb) (bc). **11** Natural History Museum, London (clb); Natural History Museum, London (ca). **12** Senckenberg, Forschungsinstitut und Naturmuseum, Frankfurt (bl). **13** Natural History Museum, London (cr). **15** Natural History Museum, London (cr) (clb -sticker). **17** Robert L. Braun -model maker (crb) (cla). **19** Natural History Museum, London (fcra); Museo Arentino de Cirendas Naterales, Buenos Aires (cra); Luis Rey -model maker (cr - velociraptor). **20** Natural History Museum, London (c) (b). **21** Natural History Museum, London (cra -apatosaurus's claw); Peabody Museum of Natural History, Yale University (cla -deinonychus). **22** Robert L. Braun -model maker (ca). **23** Royal Tyrrell Museum of Palaeontology, Alberta, Canada (crb). **27** Natural History Museum, London (cra) (fcra); Royal Tyrrell Museum of Palaeontology, Alberta, Canada (fcla) (cla). **29** American Museum of Natural History (skulls); Natural History Museum, London (clb). **30** Robert L. Braun -model maker (bl). **32** Natural History Museum, London (ca -sticker). **33** Natural History Museum, London (cra). **34** American Museum of Natural History. **36** Natural History Museum, London (clb -wild turkey feather) (bl) (br). **39** Senckenberg, Forschungsinstitut und Naturmuseum, Frankfurt (crb). **41** Natural History Museum, London (crb) (crb -feather). **43** Natural History Museum, London (bl).

Jacket images: Front: DK Images: National Guild of Stone Masons and Carvers, London cra; Luis Rey -model maker cr; Senckenberg, Forschungsinstitut und Naturmuseum, Frankfurt clb. **Back: DK Images:** Dinosaur State Park, Connecticut clb; Natural History Museum, London crb.

All other images © Dorling Kindersley
For further information see:
www.dkimages.com

PROGRESS CHART

Chart your progress as you work through the activity and quiz pages in this book.
First check your answers, then stick a gold star in the correct box below.

Page	Topic	Star	Page	Topic	Star	Page	Topic	Star
14	The birth of the dinosaurs	⭐	24	Land of the dinosaurs	⭐	34	How to rebuild a dinosaur	⭐
15	Classifying dinosaurs	⭐	25	Land of the dinosaurs	⭐	35	How to rebuild a dinosaur	⭐
16	The age of the dinosaurs	⭐	26	Hunting and scavenging	⭐	36	From dinosaur to bird	⭐
17	The age of the dinosaurs	⭐	27	Grazing dinosaurs	⭐	37	End of the dinosaur age	⭐
18	Herbivores and carnivores	⭐	28	Birth and growth	⭐	38	Dinosaur bodies	⭐
19	Dinosaur bodies	⭐	29	Birth and growth	⭐	39	Mesozoic world	⭐
20	Hands and feet	⭐	30	Other prehistoric creatures	⭐	40	Attack and defence	⭐
21	Hands and feet	⭐	31	Other prehistoric creatures	⭐	41	Dinosaur lives	⭐
22	Defence and adornment	⭐	32	Dinosaur discoveries	⭐	42	Fossil finding	⭐
23	Defence and adornment	⭐	33	Fossils	⭐	43	Dinosaur destruction	⭐

EYEWITNESS PROJECT BOOKS
DINOSAURS

CERTIFICATE OF EXCELLENCE

Congratulations to

(Name)...

for successfully completing this book on

(Award date)..